A Short Man with Tons of Change

Illustrations By Art Innovations

Vicky J. Wedel

© 2024 by Vicky J. Wedel. All rights reserved.

Published by Redemption Press, PO Box 427, Enumclaw, WA 98022 (360) 226-3488.

Redemption Press is honored to present this title in partnership with the author. The views expressed or implied in this work are those of the author. Redemption Press provides our imprint seal representing design excellence, creative content, and high-quality production.

Commercial interests: No part of this publication may be reproduced in any form, stored in a retrieval system, or transmitted in any form by any means—electronic, photocopy, recording, or otherwise—without prior written permission of the publisher/author, except as provided by United States of America copyright law.

All Scripture quotations are from the Holy Bible, New Living Translation, copyright ©1996, 2004, 2015 by Tyndale House Foundation. Used by permission of Tyndale House Publishers, Carol Stream, Illinois 60188. All rights reserved.

Illustrations by Art Innovations (https://www.artinnovations.in/).

ISBN 13 : 978-1-63232-822-9 (Paperback)
978-1-7337458-7-1 (eBook)

Library of Congress Catalog Card Number : 2024912389

A Short Man with Tons of Change

Illustrations By Art Innovations

Vicky J. Wedel

REDEMPTION PRESS

This man loved his money.

"How can you be out of bread? You just opened."

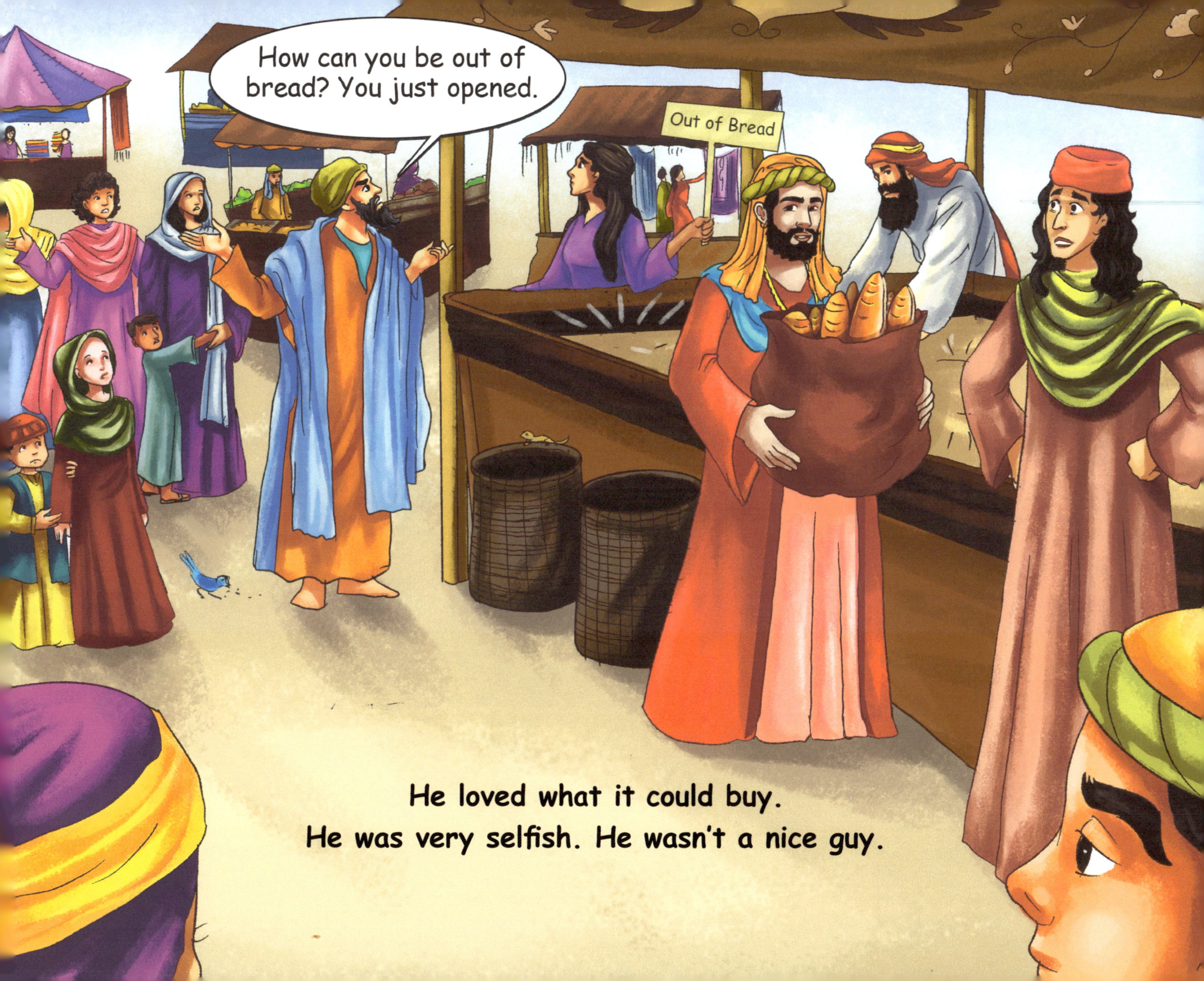

Out of Bread

He loved what it could buy.
He was very selfish. He wasn't a nice guy.

"You owe more."

But I thought...

"More..."

He was a tax collector, but he demanded more.

He didn't think of others. And he ignored the poor.

"That's Zacchaeus. We owe taxes, and he demands more than we owe."

People didn't like him because of what he did. When people saw this man, they scowled at him or hid.

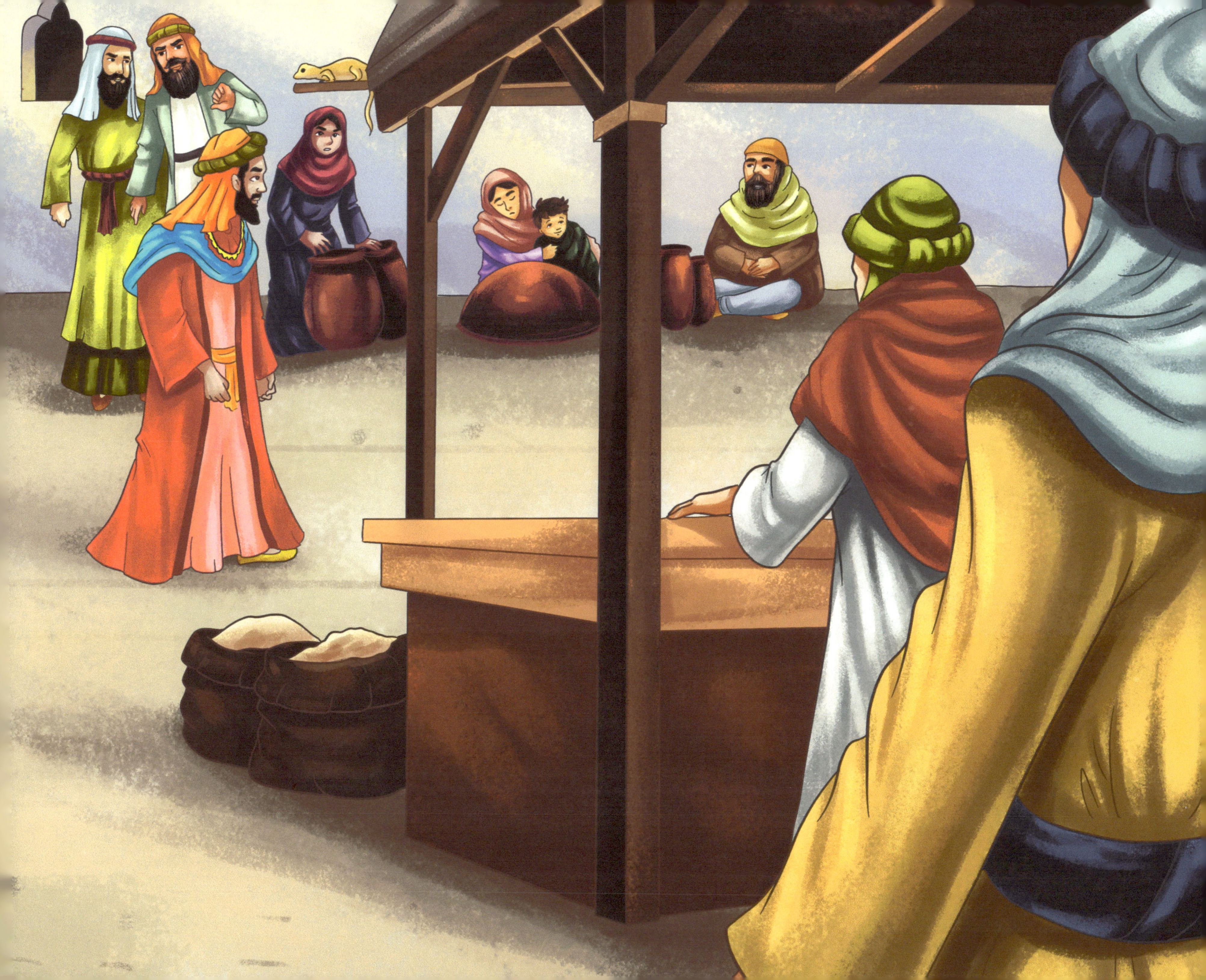

One day he saw a crowd and heard some people say,
"Jesus is in our town, and He's coming this way."

"Jesus is coming!"

This man did not know Jesus,
but Jesus knew this man.
Jesus knew all he had done
and also knew God's plan.

This man was so short that he couldn't see. So he ran ahead to climb a fig tree.

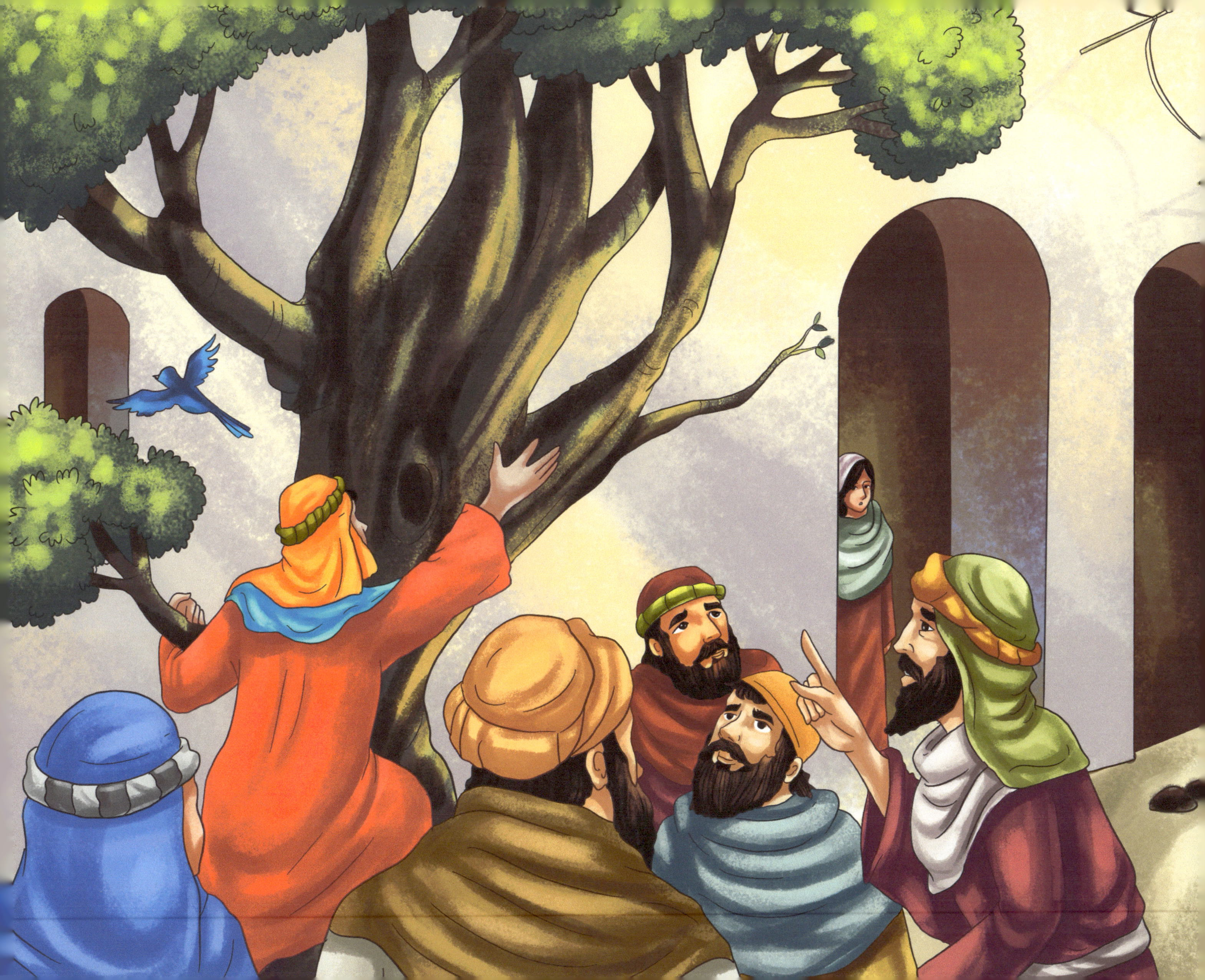

Zacchaeus, hurry and come down. I must stay at your house today.

When Jesus reached the fig tree,
He called this man by name.
He said that He would stay with him.
He said this with
no shame.

Jesus is going to be the guest of a sinner!

The crowd was so offended. They whispered their disgust.
How could Jesus stay with him, a man they could not trust?

The people had forgotten
or did not understand.
Jesus is the only One
who does all God commands.
This man hurried down the tree,
and with joy brought Jesus in.

He found he needed Jesus for a new life to begin.

His heart was full of Jesus;
he gave half to the poor.
He sought to live differently
and wanted to do more.

I heard Zacchaeus tell Jesus he'd give half to the poor and he is doing just that!
Half?!

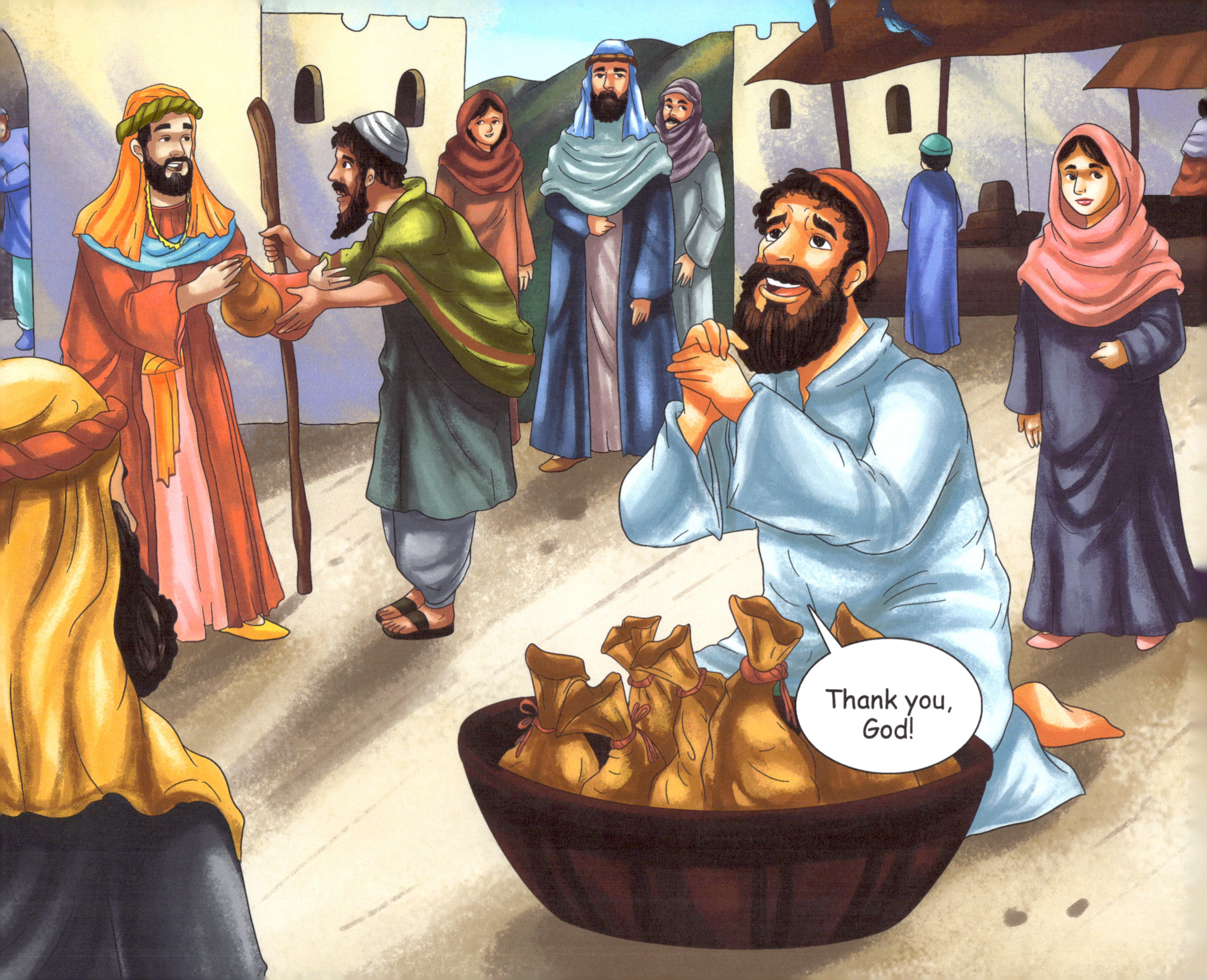
Thank you, God!

"He did what he said he would!"

He returned stolen money and paid them extra too.
His life looked very different.
His love for Jesus grew.

He was still a sinner. Sometimes he still did wrong.
But then his actions showed to Jesus he belonged.

Oh no, the old Zacchaeus is back.

I'm so sorry I lost my temper. Please forgive me. If you're willing, I want to hear what you were trying to tell me when I lost my temper.

I wonder if sometimes
he took others to the tree.
Told them about Jesus,
the Man he just had to see.

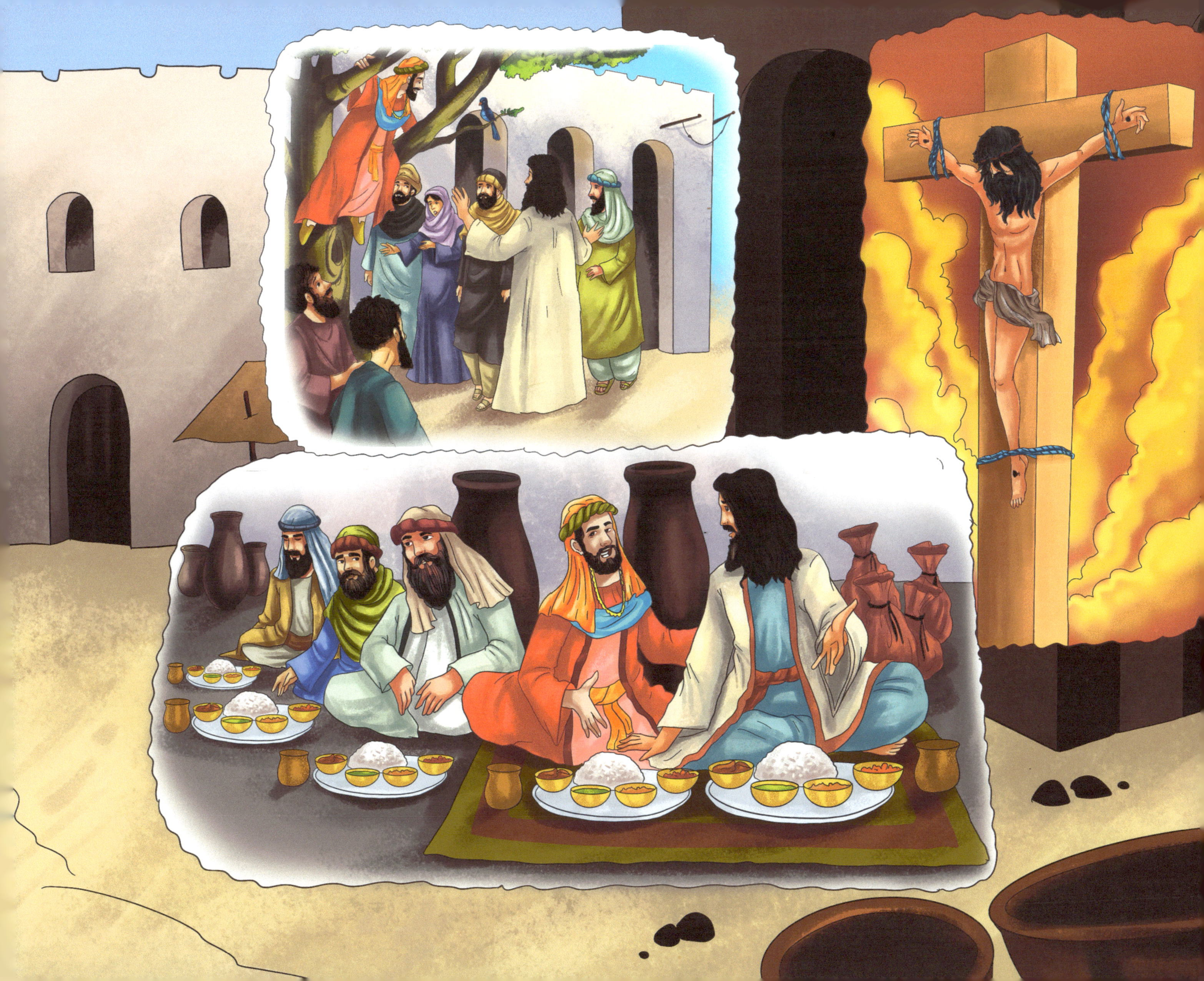

"I sure do miss him but am glad he's with Jesus."
Remember how he was before meeting Jesus?
Yes! Only God can do that!

Later on, when this man died, he had so many friends.
Now he lives in heaven, where goodness never ends.
He's so grateful Jesus came to his house to stay.
And He doesn't need a tree to see Him every day.

A MESSAGE TO READERS

The Bible tells us several things about this changed man. His name was Zacchaeus, and he lived in Jericho. The wealthy, short chief tax collector wanted to see who Jesus was (Luke 19:1–10). Since I learned more about the culture in which Zacchaeus lived, this story has become even more fascinating to me. In Zacchaeus's day, it would be considered undignified for an older man to run in public (even more so for a man who held a high position), and he would be unlikely to climb a tree at all. But something was happening within Zacchaeus for him to suddenly not care what the townspeople thought. And after meeting with Jesus, he was radically different from the selfish thief he'd been.

He told Jesus (and others in earshot) that half of all he had was going to the poor. Saying this out loud held him accountable to those who heard him. He said this in present tense as if to say, "This is as good as done." But what he said next—repaying four times what he'd stolen from others—was in future tense. Was this because it would take a while for him to earn enough money to pay what he'd promised? And why did he promise four times the amount stolen when Levitical law only required returning the amount stolen plus one-fifth of its amount to make restitution (Leviticus 6:5)? He was so heartbroken over what he'd done and filled with gratitude for Jesus's generous gift of accepting him as His own, generosity spilled out of him onto others. Jesus's loving response affirmed his faith was real: "Salvation has come to this home today, for this man has shown himself to be a true son of Abraham" (Luke 19:9–10).

God is in the business of change, changing those of us who embrace that we are sinners in need of a Savior and that Jesus is the Savior God promised (Romans 3:12, John 14:6, Genesis 3:15). With faith in Jesus, sometimes change is radical, as seen in Zacchaeus. Other times, it's gradual, but change is always promised. As our gratitude for what He's done grows in us, we begin to inwardly experience the abundant life God has promised.

ABOUT THE AUTHOR

Vicky Wedel is a follower of Christ, wife, mother, and friend. She loves sharing what God has taught her through the messiness of life. Her hope in writing is to introduce Jesus to those who haven't yet met Him and encourage those who embrace Him as Savior.

Published books:
- *The Messy Narrow Road* (forty devotionals, poems, and questions to reflect upon)
- *Being the Boss* (helping kids understand what it means to be "in charge")
- *A Short Man with Tons of Change* (the importance of making amends)
- *The Wonder at the Well* (the joy that comes from being fully known and loved)
- *Why Dogs Don't Moo* (understanding why some things won't change)

Coming soon:
- *The Weed of Unforgiveness* (learning what forgiveness is and isn't)
- *The Greatest Treasure* (learning some of the many names of Jesus)

ABOUT THE ILLUSTRATOR

Art Innovations is a dynamic and innovative illustration company that specializes in creating visually stunning and captivating illustrations for a wide range of clients. With a team of highly skilled and experienced illustrators, we bring a unique blend of creativity, passion, and expertise to every project we work on.

At Art Innovations, we believe that great illustrations have the power to bring stories to life, communicate complex ideas in a simple and engaging way, and leave a lasting impression on audiences. That's why we work closely with our clients to understand their vision and goals and then use our skills and expertise to create illustrations that exceed their expectations.

Our services include:
- *Children's Story Book illustrations*
- *Bible illustrations*
- *Scientific illustrations*
- *Line art illustrations*
- *Conceptual illustration*
- *Character design*
- *Storyboarding*
- *Product illustration*
- *and much more!*

Order Information

REDEMPTION
PRESS

Additional copies of this book can be ordered
wherever Christian books are sold.